AFRICAN HERBS FOR SEX

For Men and the Women Who Love Them

Dominion Keith

Godilian Publishing

CONTENTS

INTRODUCTION

Multiplication was a significant-good and strict issue and aphrodisiacs were looked to guarantee both male and female power. Sexual brokenness is a powerlessness to accomplish an ordinary sex, including untimely discharge, retrograded, hindered or restrained discharge, erectile brokenness, excitement troubles (diminished moxie), urgent sexual conduct, orgasmic confusion, and disappointment of detumescence. The presentation of the principal pharmacologically affirmed solution for ineptitude, Viagra (sildenafil) in the 1990s caused an influx of open consideration, moved to a limited extent by overwhelming publicizing. The quest for such substances goes back centuries. A Spanish fly is a specialist (nourishment or medication) that stirs sexual want. The chase for characteristic enhancement from restorative plants is being escalated for the most part in light of its less symptoms. In this survey, we have referenced the pharmacologically tried (either in man or creature or in both) sexual enhancer plants, which have guaranteed for its employments.

WHAT IS APHRODISIAC

A Spanish fly is characterized as any nourishment or medication that excites the sexual nature, incites general want, and expands joy and execution. This word is gotten from Aphrodite the Greek Goddess of adoration and these substances are gotten from plants, creatures, or minerals and since days of yore they have been the enthusiasm of man. A ton of common substances have truly been known as aphrodisiacs in Africa and Europe, as yohimbine and the mandrake plant, just as ground rhinoceros horn in the Chinese culture and "Spanish fly" which is poisonous. Indeed, even in the present culture, there are sure nourishments that are utilized as aphrodisiacs, including strawberries and crude shellfish. Chocolate, espresso, and nectar are likewise accepted to have Spanish fly potential. Even though these regular things are guaranteed as aphrodisiacs, there is no or minimal logical affirmation supporting those statements.

In an on-going report directed in the Boston zone, 52% of men between the ages of 40 and 70 revealed some level of erectile dysfunction (ED). Upgraded sexual conduct may give expanded relationship fulfilment and confidence in people. The chase for a compelling love potion has been a consistent interest from the beginning of time. The job of different dopaminergic, adrenergic, and serotonergic operators has been seriously analysed in both human and creature contemplates. A portion of these medications has been considered for their potential job for the treatment of sexual brokenness, while some others have added to the essential neurophysiological procedures in sexual excitement.

Aphrodisiacs can be characterized by their method of activity into three kinds: Those that expansion drive, strength, or sexual delight. Different substances of creature and plant sources have been utilized in people medications of various societies to stimulate, vitalize and improve sexual capacity, and physical execution in men, out of these not very many have been recognized pharmacologically. For expanding charisma, ambrein, a significant constituent of Ambra grisea, is utilized in Arab nations. It contains tricyclic triterpene liquor which expands the centralization of a few front pituitary hormones and serum testosterone. Bufo frog skin and organs contain bufotenine (and different bufadienolides), a psychedelic congener of serotonin. It is the dynamic fixing in West Indian "love stone" and the Chinese drug chan su. In customary Chinese medication, Panax ginseng is utilized as a sex energizer. It fills in as a cancer prevention agent by improving nitric oxide (NO) blend in the endothelium of corpora cavernosa (CC); ginsenosides likewise cause transmural nerve incitement enacted unwinding related with expanded tissue cyclic guanosine monophosphate. For expanding sexual joy, cantharidin ("Spanish fly") from rankling scarabs, which have been utilized for centuries as a sexual energizer

CHAPTER ONE

CAUSES OF IMPOTENCE

Sexual brokenness is a genuine clinical and social manifestation that happens in 10-52% of men and 25-63% of ladies. ED, the principle reason of male ineptitude, is considered as one of the most significant general medical issues, since it influences an incredible level of men. ED is characterized as the steady failure to acquire or keep up an erection for acceptable sexual relations. An expected 20-30 million men experience the ill effects of some level of sexual brokenness. It happens ordinarily in moderately aged and more seasoned men. Ineptitude happens in half of men with diabetes mellitus.

Atherosclerosis is the reason for roughly 40% of ED in men more established than 50 years. Among the most regularly perceived conditions related are hypertension, lipid issues (cholesterol, triglycerides), diabetes, and cigarette smoking. Endocrine issue like low testosterone and thyroid issues additionally adds to ED. Pelvic injury, pelvic medical procedure (significant prostate, bladder, and entrail activities) and pelvic radiation treatments are additionally associated with ED. Direct injury to the perineum can make vascular tissues in the penis and lead ED that might be treatable by penile corridor sidestep medical procedure.

Sexual brokenness is likewise brought about by different factors, for example, mental disarranges like nervousness, misery, stress, dread of sex, neurological clutters, stroke, cerebral injury, and Parkinson's malady, penile infections like phimosis. Other natural causes incorporate incessant renal disappointment, hepatic disappointment, various sclerosis, Alzheimer's malady, rest apnea, and interminable obstructive pneumonic infection. Ceaseless liquor misuse and cigarette smoking likewise unfavorably influence sexual intensity. Reduction in hormone level with age, foundational maladies like disease likewise impacts sexual capacity. ED is likewise connected with some remedial operators like antihypertensives, antipsychotics, antidepressants, and medications for diabetes mellitus

Male sexual excitement is a perplexing procedure that includes the cerebrum, hormones, feelings, nerves, muscles, and veins. Erectile brokenness can result from an issue with any of these. Moreover, stress and psychological wellness concerns can cause or intensify erectile brokenness.

Here and there a mix of physical and mental issues causes erectile brokenness. For example, a minor state of being that eases back your sexual reaction may cause nervousness about keeping up an erection. The subsequent nervousness can prompt or exacerbate erectile brokenness.

Physical reasons for erectile brokenness

Much of the time, erectile brokenness is brought about by something physical. Normal causes include:

Heart malady

Clogged veins (atherosclerosis)

High cholesterol

High circulatory strain

Diabetes

Obesity

Metabolic disorder a condition including expanded circulatory strain, high insulin levels, muscle to fat ratio around the midsection and elevated cholesterol

Parkinson's malady

Multiple sclerosis

Certain professionally prescribed meds

Tobacco use

Peyronie's malady improvement of scar tissue inside the penis

Alcoholism and different types of substance misuse

Sleep issue

Treatments for prostate malignancy or broadened prostate

Surgeries or wounds that influence the pelvic zone or spinal rope

Low testosterone

Mental reasons for erectile brokenness

The cerebrum assumes a key job in setting off the arrangement of physical occasions that cause an erection, beginning with sentiments of sexual energy. Various things can meddle with sexual emotions and cause or intensify erectile brokenness. These include:

Depression, uneasiness or other emotional well-being conditions

Stress

Relationship issues because of stress, poor correspondence or different concerns

Hazard FACTORS

As you get more established, erections may take more time to create and probably won't be as firm. You may require a more straightforward touch to your penis to get and keep an erection.

Different hazard elements can add to erectile brokenness, including:

Medical conditions, especially diabetes or heart conditions

Tobacco use, which confines bloodstream to veins and courses, can after some time cause interminable wellbeing conditions that lead to erectile brokenness

Being overweight, particularly in case you're hefty

Certain clinical medications, for example, prostate medical procedure or radiation treatment for malignancy

Injuries, especially on the off chance that they harm the nerves or supply routes that control erections

Medications, including antidepressants, antihistamines, and meds to treat hypertension, agony or prostate conditions

Psychological conditions, for example, stress, uneasiness or sorrow

Drug and liquor use, particularly in case you're a drawn-out medication client or overwhelming consumer

Inconveniences

Inconveniences coming about because of erectile brokenness can include:

An unacceptable sexual coexistence

Stress or tension

Embarrassment or low confidence

Relationship issues

The failure to get your accomplice pregnant

Stop smoking, restrict or maintain a strategic distance from liquor, and don't utilize unlawful medications.

Exercise consistently.

Take steps to decrease pressure.

Get help for tension, discouragement, or other psychological well-being concerns.

CHAPTER TWO

THE BEST HERB TO CURE LOW LIBIDO

Herbs have increased exceptional notoriety among men who need to build their sexual presentation and lift their charisma in the most recent years. Today, these common instruments are generally utilized because of their negligible symptoms, the rich substance of fundamental nutrients, and a wide scope of restorative properties.

Also, homegrown medication is a mix of uncommonly characteristic items used to improve the whole body's execution. Herbs can once in a while cause hypersensitivities and other unfavorable impacts. The principle preferred position of natural medication is that you can rehearse it at home and accomplish the alluring impact without visiting specialists frequently.

How about we examine different preferences of treating male sexual execution with herbs.

Herbs set aside your cash

It's no mystery that medication is very costly today. In any case, homegrown cures are a lot less expensive and you can get them at any medication store. This makes natural medication accessible for each man on the planet.

Sustainable outcomes

Herbs, as a rule, give you maintainable outcomes when utilized in the battle against issues identified with the male sexual exhibition. They can expand erection, forestall early discharge, and lift your sexual drive since you keep solid propensities and appropriate nourishment.

No unfavorable impacts

Herbal medication rejects practically all unfriendly impacts. Also, even on the off chance that there are any, they are normally irrelevant and, when in doubt, brought about by the ill-advised utilization of these or those herbs. Yet, conventional medications used to upgrade male sexual execution may have some unfortunate impacts, which can unfavorably influence some sexual capacities and even the whole male living being.

This book audits science-upheld aphrodisiacs that can help your charisma.

1. MACA

Maca is a sweet root vegetable with a few medical advantages. In South America it's generally used to support fruitfulness, in any event, passing by the moniker " s identified with cruciferous vegetables including broccoli, cauliflower, kale, and cabbage.

Maca is one of only a handful hardly any mainstream regular aphrodisiacs that is supported by science. Creature considers report increments in charisma and erectile capacity in mice and rodents took care of maca and maca appears to have moxie boosting impacts in people as well. Four top-notch considers detailed that members experienced upgraded sexual want after they devoured maca. Besides, a little report proposes that maca may help decrease the loss of drive that is ordinarily experienced as a reaction of certain energizer drugs. Most investigations gave 1.53.5 grams of maca every day for 212 weeks. Members for the most part endured these admissions well and experienced barely any symptoms. Be that as it may, more examinations are expected to decide safe doses and long haul impacts.

2. TRIBULUS

Tribulus terrestris, otherwise called bindii, is a yearly plant that develops in dry atmospheres. It is normally used to help improve athletic execution, barrenness, and loss of drive. This enhancement is additionally sponsored by some science. Creature considers report expanded sperm creation in rodents given Tribulus supplements. Another investigation discovered 88% of ladies with sexual brokenness experienced expanded sexual fulfillment after taking 250 mg of Tribulus for every day for 90 days. Also, a gathering of analysts inspected the impact of Tribulus in ladies with sexual brokenness by giving them 7.5 mg of the concentrate every day. Following a month, the ladies given Tribulus revealed fundamentally more significant levels of want, excitement, grease, and climax fulfillment. So, more research is expected to assess ideal dosing, just as the impacts of Tribulus supplements in men.

3. GINKGO BILOBA

Ginkgo biloba is a natural enhancement that got from perhaps the most seasoned specie of trees the Ginkgo biloba tree. It's mainstream in conventional Chinese medication as a treatment for some, infirmities, including misery and poor sexual capacity. Ginkgo biloba is said to go about as a love potion by loosening up veins and increment bloodstream. By the by, examines have delivered blended outcomes. For instance, one little examination reports that ginkgo biloba diminished the loss of moxie brought about by energizer use in around 84% of members. Both male and female members said they encountered expanded want, fervor, and capacity to climax in the wake of expending 60120 mg of the enhancement every day, although impacts appeared to be more grounded in female members. In any case, a subsequent report noticed no upgrades in a comparative gathering of members who took ginkgo biloba. Ginkgo biloba is commonly very much endured, however it might go about as a blood more slender. In this manner, in case you're taking blood-diminishing prescriptions, make a point to check with your human services proficient before taking ginkgo biloba.

4. RED GINSENG

Ginseng is another well-known herb in Chinese medication. One specific sort of red ginseng is regularly used to treat an assortment of afflictions in people, including low charisma and sexual capacity. A few examinations have explored its utilization in men and saw that red ginseng was in any event twice as compelling as the fake treatment at improving erectile capacity. Likewise, one little investigation in menopausal ladies found that red ginseng may improve sexual excitement. Be that as it may, these outcomes are not general. Additionally, a few specialists question the quality of these examinations and caution that more research is required before solid ends can be made.

One examination had members take 1.43 grams of red ginseng day by day for 412 weeks. This and another examination found that individuals by and large endure ginseng well, however it might meddle with blood-diminishing drugs and the treatment of hormone-touchy malignancies. Now and again, ginseng may likewise cause cerebral pains, clogging, or minor stomach upset.

5. FENUGREEK

Fenugreek is a yearly plant developed around the world. Its seeds are most usually utilized in South Asian dishes, but at the same time it's well known in Ayurvedic medicine as a calming, drive boosting treatment and maybe this is in light of current circumstances this herb seems to contain aggravates that the body can use to make sex hormones, for example, estrogen and testosterone.

In one little investigation, men were given 600 mg of fenugreek separate every day for about a month and a half-revealed encountering expanded sexual excitement and more climaxes. Correspondingly, a little report explored the impacts of an every-day portion of 600 mg of fenugreek extricate in ladies who had revealed having a low sex drive. It watched a huge increment in sexual want and excitement in the fenugreek bunch before the finish of the eight-week study, contrasted with the fake treatment gathering.

Fenugreek is commonly very much endured, yet can communicate with blood-diminishing prescription and may cause minor stomach upset. Besides, because of its effect on sex hormones, fenugreek may likewise meddle with the treatment of hormone-delicate diseases.

6. PISTACHIOS NUT

Individuals have been eating pistachio nuts since 6,000 BC. They are very nutritious and especially wealthy in protein, fiber, and sound fats. Pistachios may have an assortment of medical advantages, including helping lower pulse, control weight, and decrease the danger of coronary illness. Also, they may likewise help lessen manifestations of erectile brokenness.

In one little examination, men who devoured 3.5 ounces (100 grams) of pistachio nuts every day for three weeks experienced expanded bloodstream to the penis and firmer erections. Specialists have recommended these impacts might be because of the capacity of pistachios to improve blood cholesterol and invigorate better bloodstream all through the body. Be that as it may, this examination didn't utilize a fake treatment gathering, which makes it hard to decipher the outcomes. More examinations are required before solid ends can be made.

7. SAFFRON

Saffron is a flavor gotten from the Crocus sativus blossom. It is local to Southwest Asia and one of the most costly flavors by weight. This flavor is frequently utilized as an elective solution to help treat discouragement, lessen pressure and improve temperament. Also, saffron is additionally well known for its potential sexual enhancer properties, particularly in people taking antidepressants.

One investigation saw that a gathering of men given 30 mg of saffron for every day for about a month experienced more noteworthy enhancements in erectile capacity than men given a fake treatment. A subsequent report in ladies revealed that those in the saffron bunch experienced more significant levels of excitement and expanded oil, contrasted with those in the fake treatment gathering

By the by, concentrates on saffron's Spanish fly properties in people not experiencing sorrow yield conflicting outcomes

8. CISTANCHE BARK

Cistanche Bark is a significant restorative plant in customary Chinese medication and has been mainstream for a huge number of years. It is a tonic herb that improves blood dissemination and lift charisma. Cistanche has gained notoriety for expanding vitality and keeping up energy and is an extraordinary enemy of maturing herb. It is utilized to fortify the fundamental capacity of the kidney, and the sexual organs and instigate laxation, for the treatment of ineptitude and untimely discharge.

9. CNIDIUM

Cnidium seed contains a few mixes including coumarins, osthol, imperatorin, glucides, and hepatoprotective sesquiterpenes.

Cnidium seeds although not all that notable in the West are one of the best normal solutions for increment sex drive and lift charisma. It works like doctor prescribed medications to increment nitric oxide creation and hinder PDE-5. This empowers a solid erection to happen and be kept up for a longer timeframe. Cnidium as a side-effect additionally advances improved blood dissemination.

10. EPIMEDIUM GRANDIFLORUM EXTRACT "HORNY GOAT WEED"

This herb is something other than an infectious name it is one of the most significant herbs for sexual intensity in Chinese medication and has been utilized for more than 2000 years to battle erectile brokenness and lift drive. It goes about as a restoring tonic to ease weakness and diminish pressure. Studies have indicated it works in a few different ways to support male sexual execution.

To start with, horny goat weed functions as an adaptogen by expanding levels of epinephrine, norepinephrine, serotonin, and dopamine when they are low-advancing vitality and yet lessens cortisol levels when they are raised, decreasing the degree of worry in the body. High-stress conditions and expanded cortisol levels cause weariness and this, is a tremendous energy executioner.

11. SCHIZANDRA BERRY

Schizandra berries are not notable again in the West however are an old ground-breaking Chinese love potion which, are accepted to help drive and fortify the sex organs. On a psychological level, it assists battle with fatigue and stress which are the significant reason for "not being in the state of mind" which an enormous measure of men experience the ill effects of.

CHAAPTER THREE

HOW TO INCREASE LIBIDO WITH FOOD

1. Celery

While celery can barely be related to sex, this plant is viewed as one of the most helpful nourishments for male wellbeing and sexual drive. In old Greece, grapplers normally ate celery to expand their quality and continuance.

It is no mishap that specialists frequently contrast the properties of this plant and Viagra. The utilization of celery has an undeniable boosting sway on the male drive. Petioles of this plant contain a lot of the androsterone hormone, which fantastically builds the male intensity and improve their sexual drive.

2. Clams

Clams are one of the exemplary items that can normally build male moxie. It is generally utilized as a sexual promoter in numerous nations. Clams are among the items, which have the most elevated substance of zinc. No big surprise that this ocean depths upgrades the creation of male sperm and such a significant sex hormone as testosterone. Shellfish likewise supply your living being with dopamine, which splendidly animates your sexual energy.

To boost your sexual drive, clams ought to be eaten crude. Indeed, even the very procedure of eating a crude shellfish looks very sensual. The straightforward procedure of sucking in clams can assist you with accomplishing a proper sexual mind-set.

3. Bananas

Bananas can be portrayed by their rich substance of bromelain. This catalyst is accepted to support moxie and treat male erectile brokenness. Likewise, bananas can supply your living being with various basic minerals and nutrients, for example, potassium and B-bunch nutrients. For instance, riboflavin (B2) can essentially upgrade your moxie by invigorating the sexual force.

4. Avocado

In the Aztec Empire avocado was called as "ahuacatl" that signified "the gonad tree". Even though avocados did not just appear to be like this piece of the body, they additionally contain a major measure of folate (B9), which serves to appropriately process protein, in this manner giving your body essential vitality. Nutrient B6 (a supplement advancing the creation of male sex hormones) and different minerals contained in avocados can likewise help support male drive normally.

5. Almond

This nut has for some time been viewed as a magnificent supporter of male strength and moxie. It is plentiful in minerals, for example, zinc and selenium, just as in nutrient E, which assumes a significant job in fortifying the longing to sexual movement. Almonds contain various valuable fats that improve the circulatory framework, and because of the substance of Omega-3 acids, these nuts can fortify and tune the sensory system. What's more, it's simply heavenly!

6. Eggs

Although eggs are not the most sexual items, they are very plentiful in such nutrients as B6 and B5. Their substance assists with managing the degree of hormones and beat pressure. What's more, everyone realizes that these two things assume a gigantic job in boosting drive.

In numerous societies eggs have consistently been related to male ripeness and considering. A few people accept that drinking crude eggs not long before their sexual activity can support the drive, increment energy and delay the sexual delight. Eggs contain likewise such nutrients as B6 and B5, which assume an imperative job for the soundness of sperm and the whole creature.

7. Cayenne pepper

Increment erection, fortify discharge, and draw out climaxes that are the thing that ought to be referenced on the sacks of squashed red pepper. Cayenne pepper reinforces veins, extends supply routes, and improves blood flow. Its hot and rich flavor helps the affectability of erogenous zones and heats up the body.

8. Chocolate

Mixes in cacao are frequently touted to have a love potion impact, especially in ladies. Be that as it may, considers giving little proof to help this extremely mainstream thinking

9. Chasteberry

Studies propose that this natural product may impact hormone levels and lessen premenstrual disorder (PMS) manifestations in ladies. In any case, there is no proof that it offers any moxie boosting benefits

10. Nectar

It has supposedly been utilized for a considerable length of time to bring sentiment into relationships. One assortment called "distraught nectar" is even advertised as a sexual energizer. However, no examinations bolster this, and it might contain risky poisons.

11. Epimedium

Otherwise called horny goat weed, it's famous in customary Chinese medication for treating diseases like erectile brokenness. Cell and creature examine offer some early help for this utilization, however, human investigations are required.

12. HOT CHILIES

As per prevalent thinking, capsaicin, the intensify that gives hot chilies their fieriness, invigorates nerve endings on the tongue, causing the arrival of sex drive-boosting synthetic substances. Be that as it may, no examinations bolster this conviction.

CHAPTER FOUR

BEST HERBS FOR BOOSTING FEMALE SEX DRIVE

1. Ashwagandha Root

The Kama Sutra recognizes ashwagandha as an intense igniter of energy and want. While that advantage may stand out enough to be noticed, its notoriety with ladies has more to do with how it animates drive and expands fulfillment. The herb may expand bloodstream to the clitoris and other female sexual organs, making a serious sexual encounter.

2. Muira Puama

Ladies who use muira puama report a flood in drive, want, sexual pleasure, and heightened climaxes. Its beneficial outcome on both pre-and post-menopausal sexual experience underpins its general advantages for female sexual and conceptive wellbeing. It presumably does not shock anyone this herb is frequently called "power wood."

3. Dull Chocolate

This one doesn't make the rundown unintentionally. Although not a herb, dim chocolate containing 70% cocoa may help increment dopamine levels in the cerebrum. An ascent in the cerebrum's "pleasure compound" dopamine lifts the temperament, unwinds, and improves the body's reaction to incitement.

4. Avena sativa

Ages of ladies remain by oats (Avena sativa) for its Spanish fly and drive animating characteristics. Custom holds it increments vaginal incitement and advances the physical and enthusiastic wants for sex. Researchers attempting to see how it functions trust it liberates bound testosterone, furnishing the body with the hormones required for sexual incitement.

5. Catuaba

The Tupi clan of Brazil acclaims catuaba for its strong Spanish fly characteristics. Its dynamic compound yohimbine empowers and animates drive and want. Research has decided it builds dopamine levels in the mind, bringing about more noteworthy affectability to erogenous incitement. Normal use is known to make sensual dreams and increase sexual fulfillment and climax force.

6. Damiana

Turnera diffusa, also called damiana, develops locally in the American Southwest, Mexico, the Caribbean, and South America. Many consider its leaf a profoundly prized moxie enhancer. Flavonoids, phenolics, glycosides, terpenoids, and even caffeine all add to diminished sentiments of stress and expanded bloodstream, especially to the pelvic region where expanded affectability prompts elevated incitement.

7. Suma root

Now and then called Brazilian Ginseng, this herb is amazingly mainstream with the local populace in South America for how it helps female hormonal parity and energizes moxie. Science has affirmed suma root expands levels of estradiol-17beta, the essential estrogen hormone during a lady's regenerative years. Ladies who utilize this herb report increasingly exceptional sexual encounters and more noteworthy fulfillment.

8. Tribulus terrestris

Investigations of ladies who utilize this herb report more prominent want, expanded excitement, oil, increasingly extraordinary climaxes, and fulfillment. Tribulus invigorates androgen receptors in the cerebrum making the body significantly more receptive to testosterone and other sex hormones. It additionally assists with decreasing pressure, tension, and discouragement.

9. Tongkat Ali

Called the best common Spanish fly by Dr. Oz, Tongkat ali separate has been utilized by ladies to stimulate want and increment erogenous affectability. It's customarily given to ladies experiencing low moxie, as it likewise underpins positive reactions to stretch and animates memory and generally cerebrum work. By normalizing hormone levels with a delicate increment of testosterone, ladies additionally experience expanded digestion and a simpler time losing and looking after weight

CHAPTER FIVE

AFRICAN HERB FOR SEXUAL IMPROVEMENT

1.Cattle stick or poor man's light (Carpolobia lutea)

Carpolobia lutea, regularly called dairy cattle stick or poor man's flame has a place with the plant family Polygalaceae. The normal names, which the plant is known incorporate dairy cattle stick (English), Abekpok Ibuhu (Eket), Ikpafum, Ndiyan, Nyayanga (Ibibio), Agba or Angalagala (Igbo) and Egbo oshunshun (Yoruba).

Aftereffects of an examination distributed in the Journal of Intercultural Ethnopharmacology recommend that methanol concentrate on Carpolobia lutea root (MECLR) upgrades male sexual movement perhaps by enlarging nitric oxide focus.

The examination gives a novel logical justification to the utilization of Carpolobia lutea in the administration of penile erectile brokenness and weakened charisma.

2. Nutmeg (Myristica fragrans)

The dried part of comprehensively ovoid seeds of Myristica fragrans (Nutmeg) of the family Myristicaceae has been referenced in Unani medication to be of significant worth in the administration of male sexual issue. In an investigation by Tajuddin et al., it was discovered that organization of 50 percent ethanolic concentrate of a solitary portion of Nutmeg and Clove, and Penegra brought about the expansion in the mating execution of the mice. It was discovered that out of six control creatures just two guys mated (inseminated) two females and the staying four guys mated one female each during the overnight test time frame. While, Nutmeg treated male creatures mated three females each except for two, which mated five females each. In the Clove treated male creatures three mated two females every, two mated four females each and staying one mated three females each. In the Penegra treated creatures four mated five females each and two mated three females each.

3. Date palm (Phoenix dactylifera, dabino in Hausa)

Phoenix dactylifera (date palm) of the family Palmae is a local to North Africa that has been widely developed in Arabia and the Persian Gulf. The date palm dust (DPP) is utilized in the customary medication for male barrenness. In a test concentrate by Bahmanpour et al. explored the impact of P. dactylifera, dust, on sperm parameters, and conceptive arrangement of grown-up male rodents. They saw that the utilization of DPP suspensions improved the sperm tally, motility, morphology, and Deoxy Nucleic Acid (DNA)/hereditary material quality with an attendant increment in the loads of testis and epididymis.

4. Tropical almond (Terminalia catappa)

Terminalia catappa is a huge tropical tree has a place with the family, Combretaceae a noteworthy sexual enhancer potential. Ratnasooriya et al. seen that T. catappa seeds at a portion of 1500 mg/kg or 3000 mg/kg, per oral for seven days in rodents had a checked improvement of love potion activity, sexual energy. Interestingly, the higher portion (3 000 mg/kg, p.o.) reversibly restrained all the parameters of sexual conduct other than mounting.

Late investigations have indicated that diabetes and it's specialist entanglements (erectile brokenness/untimely discharge, leg ulcer/gangrene, liver/kidney disappointment), lung malignancy, and sickle cell iron deficiency can be tended to with concentrates of Indian almond. Nigerian and Indian specialists have recovered the pancreas with Indian almond separates accordingly helped glucose guideline, improved sexual and liver/kidney works in diabetics.

As indicated by an examination distributed in the Asian Journal of Andrology, male rodents were orally treated with 1500 mg/kg or 3000 mg/kg SS or vehicle, and their sexual conduct was checked three hours after the fact utilizing a responsive female. Another gathering of rodents was orally treated with either 3000 mg/kg SS or vehicle for seven continuous days. Their sexual conduct and ripeness were assessed on days one, four, and seven of treatment and day seven post-treatment by blending for the time being with a star oestrous female. The estrous cycle contains the common physiologic changes that are instigated by regenerative hormones in most mammalian placental females.

The outcomes demonstrated the 1500 mg/kg portion, had a

checked love potion activity (prolongation of discharge inactivity) however no impact on moxie sexual want (percent mounting, percent intromission, and percent discharge), sexual life (mounting-and-intromission recurrence), or sexual execution (intercopulatory interim).

Interestingly, the higher portion (3000 mg/kg) reversibly hindered all the parameters of sexual conduct other than mounting-and-intromission recurrence and copulatory effectiveness. The impacts of high portion SS were not because of general poisonous quality, liver danger, haemotoxicity, stress, muscle inadequacy, muscle incoordination, absence of pain, hypoglycemia (decreased glucose), or decrease in blood testosterone level. They were because of checked sedation.

The specialists inferred that the bit of T. catappa seeds have love potion action and might be valuable in the treatment of specific types of sexual deficiencies, for example, untimely discharge. "The current discoveries show that seeds of T. catappa have intense love potion movement and give logical proof for the cases made in Ayurvedic medication in Sri Lanka in regards to this activity. The outcomes additionally recommend that moderate utilization of a portion of the seed of T. catappa could be valuable in the treatment of men with sexual dysfunctions coming about essentially from untimely discharge."

5. Goat head (Tribulus terrestris)

Tribulus terrestris is a blossoming plant in the family Zygophyllaceae. It is ordinarily called villain's thistle, cut vine, caltrop, yellow vine, and goat head. It is a typical herb in Nigeria.

To the French, it is Croix de Malte and Abrolhos in Portuguese. In Nigeria, it is dareisa in Arabic-Shuwa, tsaiji in Fula-Fulfulde, hana taakama in Hausa (forestalls swagger, in implication to its thistles puncturing the feet-a typical statement) or tsaida (to stop provided that a thistle penetrates the foot one must stop to separate it), kaije in Kanuri, tedo by the Koma individuals of Adamawa State and da ogun daguro in Yoruba.

Organization of Tribulus terrestris (TT) to people and creatures improves drive and spermatogenesis. Neychev et al. explored the impact of T. terrestris removal on androgen digestion in youthful guys. The discoveries of study foresee that T. terrestris steroid saponins have neither direct nor roundabout androgen-expanding properties.

It is likewise found to build the degrees of testosterone, leutinizing hormone, dehydroepiandrosterone, dihydrotestosterone, and dehydroepiandrosterone sulfate. The corpus cavernosal tissues got from New Zealand White bunnies following treatment with TT were tried in vitro with different pharmacological specialists and electrical field incitement and was found to have a genius erectile impact. An investigation by Gauthaman et al. indicated the androgen discharging property of the TT concentrate and its connection to sexual conduct and intracavernous pressure utilizing maimed rodents.

6. Fadogia agrestis (bakin gagai in Hausa)

Fadogia agrestis has a place with the plant family, Rubiaceae. It is called bakin gagai in Hausa, from gagai meaning love potion. It has huge sexual enhancer potential. Yakubu et al. assessed the

Spanish fly capability of the watery concentrate of F. agrestis in Male rodents. Their sexual conduct parameters and serum testosterone fixation were assessed.

The outcomes demonstrated a critical increment in Mount Frequency (MF), Intromission recurrence (IF), and fundamentally delayed the ejaculatory dormancy and decreased mount and Intromission Latency (IL). There was additionally a noteworthy increment in serum testosterone fixations in all the gatherings in a way reminiscent of portion reliance. The fluid concentrate of F. agrestis stem expanded the blood testosterone fixations and this might be the instrument answerable for its Spanish fly impacts and different manly behaviors. It might be utilized to alter debilitated sexual capacities in creatures, particularly those emerging from hypotestosteronemia.

Yakubu et al. examined the impacts of the organization of the fluid concentrate of F. agrestis stem on some testicular capacity records of male rodents. Contrasted and the control, extricate organization for 28 days at all the dosages brought about a critical increment in the rate testicles bodyweight proportion, testicular cholesterol, sialic corrosive, glycogen, corrosive phosphatase and g-glutamyl transferase exercises while there was a huge lessening in the exercises of testicular basic phosphatase, corrosive phosphatase, glutamate dehydrogenase and convergences of protein.

7. Velvet bean or Cowhage (Mucuna pruriens, werepe in Yoruba and agbala in Ibo)

Another examination distributed a year ago in BioMed Research International distinguished Mucuna pruriens as one of the plants utilized for the development of sexual execution and virility.

Mucuna pruriens has a place with the plant family Leguminosae. The velvet bean plant is infamous for the spiky hairs on the develop bean units that are extremely bothering to the skin.

Analysts have demonstrated that Mucuna pruriens upgrades fruitfulness by delivering a portion subordinate increment in follicle invigorating hormone and luteinizing hormone which thusly expanded the number of eggs discharged at ovulation conceivably through its rich wellspring of L-Dopa and its metabolite, dopamine.

The complete alkaloids from the seeds of M. pruriens were found to build spermatogenesis and weight of the testicles, original vesicles, and prostate in the pale-skinned person rodent.

M. pruriens animated sexual capacity in typical male rodents which was seen by an increment in mounting recurrence, intromission recurrence, and discharge inactivity.

M. pruriens seed powder improved altogether different sexual parameters copulatory conduct including mount recurrence, mount inactivity, intromission recurrence, and intromission dormancy of the male pale-skinned person rodents. The ethanolic concentrates of M. pruriens seed delivered a noteworthy and supported increment in the sexual movement of ordinary male rodents at a specific portion (200mg/kg). There is altogether expanded mounting recurrence, intromission recurrence, and ejaculation inactivity and diminished mounting idleness, intromission dormancy, postejaculatory interim, and inter-intromission interim.

In clinical investigations, the treatment with M. pruriens seeds expanded sperm focus and motility in all the barren investigation bunches in man. After the treatment of concentrate the original plasma of all the fruitless gatherings, the degrees of lipids, cell reinforcement nutrients, and remedied fructose were recuperated after a lessening in lipid peroxides after treatment Their was recouped sperm focus altogether in oligo-zoospermic patients, however, sperm motility was not reestablished to ordinary levels in asthenozoospermia men.

M. pruriens essentially improved T, luteinizing hormone (LH), dopamine, adrenaline, and noradrenaline levels, and decreased degrees of follicle animating hormone (FSH) and prolactin (PRL) in barren men. It likewise essentially recouped sperm check and motility. M. pruriens treatment to fruitless men directs steroidogenesis and improves semen quality. Treatment with M. pruriens altogether hindered lipid peroxidation, raised spermatogenesis, and improved sperm motility of fruitless male and improved the degrees of all-out lipids, triglycerides, cholesterol, phospholipids, and nutrient A, C, and E and revised fructose in fundamental plasma of barren men.

M. pruriens altogether enhanced mental pressure and fundamental plasma lipid peroxide levels alongside improved sperm tally and motility. Treatment additionally reestablished the degrees of Comparison of Seminal Superoxide Dismutase (SOD), catalase, glutathione (GSH), and ascorbic corrosive in fundamental plasma of fruitless men. It reactivates the cancer prevention agent resistance arrangement of barren men and helps in the administration of stress and improves semen quality.

ABOUT THE AUTHOR

Dominion Keith

Dominion Keith is an African base scientist who specialise in developing therapeutic cure from African herbs. Her several years of experince made her an authority in this fied